Zaragoza and Aragon

A vitaminized supplement to classic tourist guides

Version 2019

Cristina & Olivier Rebière

TABLE OF CONTENTS

Thank you for purchasing this eBook and welcome to your new **"Travel eGuide**: Zaragoza and Aragon". We hope that it will help you to discover this beautiful region of Spain, located in an exceptional natural setting, crossed by the Ebro, with mountains, valleys, lakes and varied landscapes, and the beautiful Zaragoza, city of architecture and history with a rich heritage. Discover the castles of Aragon, built in Moorish architecture, the roads slaloming among pine forests, olive and almond trees, but also authentic little medieval jewels, such as Ainsa and Alquézar.

This paperback is made after an ebook you can have for free on your smartphone or Kindle (see at the end of the book the modality on how you can have it) and where you can use all the facilities explained in the next sections : "How to use this guide", and contains also the fully functional features called GeoNav, PhotoNav and IcoNav.. The ebook Travel eGuide proposes you a different approach of the journey, between a "log book" and a classic guide. You can discover hidden treasures and browse freely through all the pages.

We don't have a team like "Lonely Planet" or other big publish houses, so you are not going to find in this eGuide a large choice of accommodations, restaurants or shops. We share with you our travels, our experiences, our impressions. We hope that this will help you to discover new destinations and make you wish to visit them.

Have a great trip !

Sincerely,
Cristina & Olivier

Spain - practical tips

Budget tips:

Depending on your country of origin, the tips can be different to have cheaper flight tickets.
Here are some advice which apply, no matter where you are coming from.

Buy your tickets in advance (3 months minimum) to get the best rates so you can choose the dates of your vacation. Look for promotions from different airlines. Do not buy your tickets at once, but "test" the market first. Look for the airline companies which flies to Spain: Madrid, Barcelona or Zaragoza http://www.zaragoza-airport.com/en/. Buy your tickets to one of these cities and then prepare your route or itinerary according to it.

Pay attention because the tickets prices may vary on every hour and without any logic. Consequently, record in a file on your computer the prices you have found for several days before making your decision. This way, you can compare and know immediately when you will have an opportunity not to be missed. You can save more than 200 €/ticket in this way. If possible, avoid traveling at holiday times (Christmas, New Year, etc.) to get the cheapest price for your airline tickets. If you however wish to go during these periods, put your departure a few days before those events. According to your departure point, try the following airline companies to have more chances to obtain the best rates: **Alitalia, KLM, Iberia**, but also *lowcost* companies as **Easyjet, Ryanair, Wizz Air, Blue Air**.

If you live in Europe, you can travel by bus, which is much cheaper than the plane. You can get rates from 15 € with companies like **Flixbus, Eurolines, Ouibus**. As you probably know, Spain is a very visited country, so tourists are present almost throughout the year. The seaside resorts are crowded during the summer season, while cities with a strong cultural and artistic character like Barcelone, Madrid or Cordoba are visited in all seasons. Best time to visit the region are the summer and fall months. Temperatures are almost never negative and summer temperatures range from 20 to 33°C.

Traveling

Tips: A car rental is the most suitable way of getting around and discovering Spain. You can rent one at the airport if you arrive by plane, otherwise the roads are very good and you can arrive easily by the road..

Warning: you have to guarantee your rental with a credit card. If you have not booked through the Internet with insurance included, you may have surprises once there because the note could be higher.

Speed limits:
In Spain the speed limits are as follows:
- ☞ Urban areas : 50 km/h.
- ☞ Out of town, on single-carriageway roads: 90 km/h,
- ☞ Roads for automobiles of « vía rápida » type: 100 km/h.
- ☞ On motorways ("autopista") and expressways (« autovía »): 110 or 120 km/h

Obligation to have 2 pre-signaling triangles (1 for the front of the car, one for the rear), a fluorescent vest and a box of spare bulbs. Attention, you can have fines in case of absence of these articles in the vehicle.

Accommodation

There are several types of accommodation in Spain, from apartment rentals to hotels, hostels and campsites. It all depends on your budget and how many people travel together.

Tips: If you travel with children or with friends, the most economical alternative is the holiday rentals. The price of this type of accommodation is cheaper than hotel room rates and starts from 40 € / night for an apartment that can accommodate 4 people.

Food & gastronomy

During your trip in Spain, you can discover in addition to its magnificent landscapes, the rich gastronomy of this country. Gourmets can enjoy tapas, delicacies and stews, meat and fish dishes, soups and exquisite desserts. For more details on the local cuisine and some typical recipes of Aragon see at the end of the book the section « Gastronomy ».

How to use the *eGuide?*

You have already read dozens of books or travel guides in your life. They usually have a table of contents at the beginning and either an index, glossary or an acknowledgement section at the end.

The electronic version of this guide contains a lot of this information, but it also has an added bonus that will help you to quickly and intuitively mobilize the content and personalize your reading mode: it is a true digital touch-screen eBook, a kind of website that doesn't need an Internet connection. We organized this eGuide in a conventional way for those who want to read "normally" without asking any metaphysical or methodological questions: if you want, you can jump directly to "The places to visit". For the curious or "computer savvy", here are the three modes of navigation that we offer. You can always go back while reading using the button "Back" on your smartphone, tablet or touch screen computer.

A top horizontal menu with 3 icons

At the top-right hand corner of every page there is a horizontal menu bar with three round "floating" icons. They are tagged **"GeoNAV"**, **"PhotoNAV"** and **"IcoNAV"**. Each of their functions is described below.

All underlined texts are hyperlinks: therefore, you can click on them on the electronic version. Below is an example of the hyperlinks that you can touch and activate (circled in red): On the left, under the menu bar and the name of the section you're reading, you can see colorful thematic icons, as a square, with a symbol inside. On the left, under the menu bar and the name of the section you're reading, you can see colorful thematic icons, as a square, with a symbol inside. Here are some examples:

These icons announce clearly and simply the points of interest which are present in the respective section. The background color of the icons depends on the theme. You can see the details of these icons in the IcoNAV chapter.

At the top right, you can see THREE round navigation icons with a dark pictogram inside. Here is a detailed explanation:

1. GeoNAV: a "classic" geographical exploration

By clicking the hypertext link (or hyperlink) located immediately below this round compass-styled icon, you reach a "classic" view of the map, displaying colored geographical areas and hyperlinks next to the map that allow you to access the respective chapter with a simple click. In the electronic version you can select and read about the different places of interest you want to find out about.

2. PhotoNAV: discover the locations by photos

By clicking the hyperlink on the electronic version, located immediately below this round camera-styled icon, you can view photos taken by me or made available by the authors on Wikipedia (whom I make reference to and thank at the end of the book) in order to discover the beauty of this country. So, if you like a picture, click on it (or on the hyperlink below) and go directly to the respective tourist attractions!

3. IcoNAV: choose your points of interest or hobbies by icons

On the electronic version, by clicking the hyperlink located below this round question-mark styled icon on a black background, you will view the list of all the points of interest, or "icons" presented in this e-guide. In the paper version, you can see the destinations concerned by the icon and go directly to read all the details. Within the "IcoNAV" chapter, you will view the thematic icons, and for each of them, its respective list of attractions, listed as hyperlinks, which you can activate by clicking on the electronic version. It couldn't be any easier!

How to view the maps?

If you wish to have the electronic version and are not connected to the Internet and if your eBook reader allows it, you can zoom in (with your mouse wheel or by spreading two fingers apart on your touch screen device) because their resolution allows to do so. If you have Internet access you can also access the proposed website "OpenStreetMap" by clicking or touching on the hyperlink (circled here in red) located immediately below the respective map.

GeoNAV

In the electronic version, you can browse your Travel eGuide by choosing your desired location on the map.

Aragon, 4 tourist sections

PhotoNAV

In the electronic version, you can browse your eGuide by choosing your desired photo and touch it with your finger in order to "jump" directly in the dream location where it was taken from!

My favorite photos

Palace of Aljaferia - Zaragoza

Coso de La Misericordia - Zaragoza

Alquézar   Ainsa

IcoNAV

In the electronic version you can browse your Travel eGuide by choosing your points of interest or hobbies by icons. Just click or touch the hypertext link (or hyperlink) located next to the thematic icon and go directly to the section!

In this paper version you can find the location on the table of contents.

"Travel eGuide" and general information icons:

CRUSH: A location which I liked a lot and that I recommend to you! Zaragoza | Huesca | Alquézar, Ainsa, Barbastro

CHILDREN: This location may interest you if you have children. Zaragoza | Huesca | Teruel

TRICK: A good idea which may interest you! Zaragoza | Huesca | Alquézar, Ainsa, Barbastro | Teruel

IMPRESSIONS: Our feelings and impressions about the location   Zaragoza

"Water" icons:

BATHING: Take your swimsuits! Alquézar, Ainsa, Barbastro

BATHING: Take your swimsuits Alquézar, Ainsa, Barbastro

"Culture" icons:

ART-CULTURE: A location with an artistic or cultural interest. Zaragoza | Alquézar, Ainsa, Barbastro | Teruel

ARCHITECTURE Zaragoza | Huesca | Alquézar, Ainsa, Barbastro | Teruel

CASTLE   Zaragoza | Huesca | Alquézar, Ainsa, Barbastro

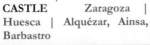

MUSEUM Zaragoza | Huesca | Alquézar, Ainsa, Barbastro | Teruel

RUINS   Zaragoza | Huesca

RELIGIOUS MONUMENT Zaragoza | Huesca | Alquézar, Ainsa, Barbastro | Teruel

"Nature" icons:

GARDEN, PARK Zaragoza | Huesca

HIKE: A site of departure / arrival of a hike Alquézar, Ainsa, Barbastro | Teruel

NATURAL WONDER: A remarkable natural site Huesca

LANDSCAPE Zaragoza | Huesca | Alquézar, Ainsa, Barbastro

"Sport" icons:

CLIMBING   Alquézar, Ainsa, Barbastro

"Leisure activities and life on-the-spot" icons:

ACCOMMODATION
Zaragoza | Huesca |
Alquézar, Ainsa, Barbastro

LEISURE PARK   Teruel

RESTAURANT Zaragoza |
Huesca | Alquézar, Ainsa,
Barbastro

SHOPPING, SOUVENIRS
Zaragoza

BUDGET   Zaragoza | Huesca | Alquézar, Ainsa, Barbastro

Aragon

Aragon is an autonomous community located in the north of Spain, made up of three provinces: the province of Huesca, the province of Zaragoza and the province of Teruel. Bordered to the north by the southern Pyrenees and to the south by the Iberian mountains, Aragon is crossed by the Ebro river and its variety of landscapes make all the charm of this region: large desert areas or with vast meadows, high mountainous peaks, lakes, green valleys. You will go from surprise to surprise!

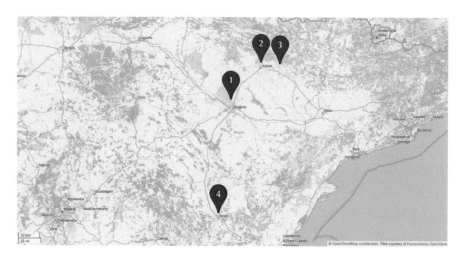

1. Zaragoza
3. Alquézar, Ainsa, and Barbastro

2. Huesca and Jaca
4. Teruel

1. Zaragoza

Zaragoza (or Saragossa) is a city in northeastern Spain, capital of the province of the same name and of Aragon. It is located 315 km northeast of Madrid and almost the same distance west of Barcelona.

To get to Zaragoza we went through large, arid, and almost desert areas with wide ocher plains burned by the sun. The landscapes seem lunar, dotted with some brushes... Only the road reminds us that we are still on Earth. Then cereal fields alternate with farms breeding pigs or cows. Far on the horizon, hills and mountains can be seen ... Then, when entering the city, the silhouette of the majestic cathedral captivates the gaze and holds it back...

Photo 1.1: On the road...

Zaragoza is a beautiful city with wide boulevards, wide sidewalks, beautiful churches and a charming historic center. A real crush that will make you travel through history, from the Romans till today.

8

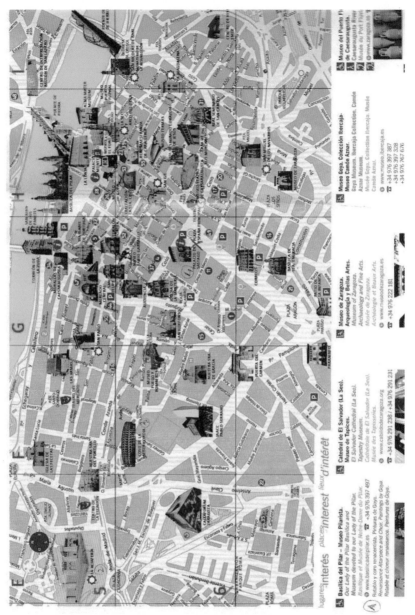

The map you will get from the Tourist Office (on Spanish place)

hoto 1.2: The Pilar Basilica and the Ebro Bridge

I recommend you visiting the city in August as we did because the locals are on vacation and even if there are tourists, the city is very nice to walk through, especially in the morning. If you are driving, I advise you to park in Calle Asalto which leads to Piazza San Miguel as you will be able to find free places along the boulevard. Very convenient :-)

You can start your tour by following *Calle Asalto*. You arrive quickly at the church of *San Miguel de los Navarros*, built in red brick in Baroque style and flanked by a beautiful tower in Mudejar style with three floors. A beautiful statue of the angel who is killing by sword a monster with a human head overcomes the portal of the church. Next door is the city hall.

Continuing on *Calle San Miguel* and taking left on *Calle Sanco* you will come to a beautiful square: *Plaza de los Sitios*. A small park is in the middle of the square which is surrounded by beautiful buildings including the Museum of Zaragoza, in New-Renaissance style; that houses collections of archeology, fine arts, ethnology and ceramics. In the middle of the square there is a stone and bronze monument, surrounded by fountains, dedicated to the defenders of the city. There is also a playground for children and benches to enjoy the shade of the big trees of the place. Another magnificent building is the *Grupo Escolar Gascón y Marín*, built at the beginning of the 20th century with Renaissance-inspired architecture.

Photo 1.4: Zaragoza museum

Then you can continue your walk along the *Calle Joaquin Costa* and arrive at the place Sainte-Engrâce and its beautiful church *Iglesia Basílica de Santa Engracia* with its magnificent portal that dates back from the old monastery Jerónimo Saint-Engrace, built in the 16th century, in Renaissance style.

Then you can continue on the large *Paseo Independencia* boulevard bordered by beautiful houses with arcades under which there are plenty of shops for shopping lovers. This major axis of the city starts at the Spanish Place and ends at *Plaza de Paraíso*, passing by the *Plaza de Aragón*. One of the prettiest buildings to see is the big post office of the city *Edificio de Correos*.

Photo 1.7: Coso de La Misericordia

At the Spanish place, I advise you to enter the Tourist Office and take a map of the city with the main things to see as it will greatly facilitate your orientation in the city. Then take the beautiful pedestrian street *Calle del Coso* with at the end the palace **Palacio de los Condes de Morata o de Luna,** built in the 16th century, in Renaissance style with a large portal. wood flanked by the bronze statues of Hercules and Theseus. Inside the palace there is a large patio and upstairs you will find a superb gallery with columns. Continuing on the *Calle del Conde de Aranda*, you will arrive at *Plaza de Toros in La Misericordia* and will be able to see the magnificent bullring there.

Less than a kilometer to the northwest following the indicators, you can go to see the magnificent Aljaferia Palace, an 11th century fortification from the time of Al-Muqtadir, built as the residence of Banu Hud kings in Zaragoza. It is a great building of Islamic architecture in Spain at the time of Taifas. The palace has undergone transformations over the centuries. The oldest building of the palace is its 9th century square Trouvere Tower with 5 floors. The interior has features of Muslim architecture and the ceilings are painted with Mudejar geometric patterns. It was a guard tower but also served as a prison in the 15th century. The palace is imposing by its size and the visit is worth it! Beautiful porticoes adorn the different parts of the palace and there is even a small mosque with refined decorations. The Patio of Santa Isabell has a lot of charm and constituted the "center" of the palace. Beautiful arcades surround the patio which is a green oasis, harmonious among the stones. The church of St. Martin is located at the northeast corner of the walls and was built in the fourteenth century, mixing the Gothic and Mudejar styles.

Photo 1.8: Aljaferia Palace

Passing through the Plaza de Europa you can then go to the

Plaza San Pablo by stopping by the pretty Piazza Santo Domingo and than by the beautiful church of San Pablo, a superb example of 14th century Gothic-Mudejar architecture that has grown over the centuries. A magnificent octagonal Mudejar tower is flanked by two smaller towers. The interior is decorated and the chapels are painted or decorated with polychrome woodwork and the altarpiece is carved in gilded wood.

Photo 1.9: Santo Domingo square

Photo 1.11: Roman wall and San Juan church

Taking on the left, you will arrive at the central market of the city in a beautiful building of the twentieth century where you can make a small gourmet stop among the specialties of the region, cold cuts, cheeses, but also vegetables and fresh fruits, meat, fish, etc. If you are hungry, you can enjoy the terraces in front of the market. We tried the Mercado Café and ate a full and decent menu for less than fifteen euros with water or wine included. In front of the market, you have the remains of the Roman wall of Zaragoza, built between the 1st and 3rd centuries around the colony of **Caesaraugusta**. This wall was more than 3,000 meters long and had about 120 defense towers. In front stands the statue of Caesar and behind there is a beautiful church - *Iglesia de San Juan de los Panetes* from the 16th to the 18th century in Baroque style. You will then arrive at the most important square in Zaragoza - Plaza del Pilar with the majestic Basilica de Nuestra Señora del Pilar, dedicated to the Virgin of Pilar, Patroness of the Civil Guard and Hispanity. The construction is impressive, with 160 meters long and 67 meters wide. It occupies the entire length of the square, overlooking the Ebro River. Crowned with 11 domes, some decorated with beautiful mosaics, the basilica has also 10 lanterns and 4 towers. Its construction began in the 17th century and lasted more than 2 centuries. Several architectural styles are present and intermingle harmoniously: Roman, Gothic, Mudejar and Baroque. On the square there is also the City Hall - Ayuntamiento , the Fountain of Hispanity and the Cathedral of St. Savior, also called the Seo. The cathedral was also built in several stages from the 12th to the 18th century, also combining several styles: Roman, Gothic, Renaissance, Mudejar, Baroque and Neoclassical. The interior of the two churches is also worth a visit as they are richly decorated with paintings, sculptures and magnificent altarpieces.

Photo 1.12: Square of Basilique de Nuestra Señora del Pilar

Photo 1.13: Basilica de Nuestra Señora del Pilar

If you want to continue your visit of the Roman vestiges, the museum of the forum is under the cathedral of San Salvador and the access is by the prism of the place. Not too far away you will find the Roman Theater of Caesaraugusta built in the first century with a capacity of 6,000 places. You can see the ruins and even visit the museum. Not far away are the Roman baths but they are only visible if you visit their museum. Always nearby, for art lovers, there is the Goya Museum which houses paintings and engravings as well as temporary exhibitions.

Photo 1.14: Roman Theater of Caesaraugusta

If you want to stay and spend the night in Zaragoza, you can choose either a pension or an apartment. You can have a double room for 30 € per night not far from center like Pensión Lacasta which is 200 meters from the Aljafería Palace with clean rooms. Otherwise there is also an Ibis Budget: a fifteen minutes walk from the center with parking and double room from 40

€ / night.

If you want to eat in the city center, not far from the Roman Theater, in the street Calle Estebanes there is a typical small restaurant, La Migueria where you can have menus at ten euros at noon with migas - a Spanish dish with bread and various accompaniments. Always in the area, in Calle Santiago at nr. 27 there is another good address: Restaurante Taberna De Alex with tapas, grills, salads and full menus for less than 17€.

Photo 1.15: Zaragoza

If you are traveling with children, a museum that might please them is the firefighters one - Museo del Fuego y los Bomberos located in Santiago Ramón y Cajal street. The first Sunday of the month admission is free, the other days adults pay a little more than 3 € and children and young people have a reduced rate. Children under 8 years old enter free of charge. Otherwise there is also the Aquarium of Zaragoza in the Avda. José Atarés is the largest river aquarium in Europe with over a hundred species of fish divided into 5 zones: the Nile, Amazon, Ebre, Mekong and Murray-Darling.

2. Huesca and Jaca

Huesca is a city in the north of Spain, capital of the province of the same name, in Aragon, located 74 km north of Zaragoza and 400 km northeast of Madrid. It is a small town that is worth a visit and you can spend one or two hours in its lively streets.

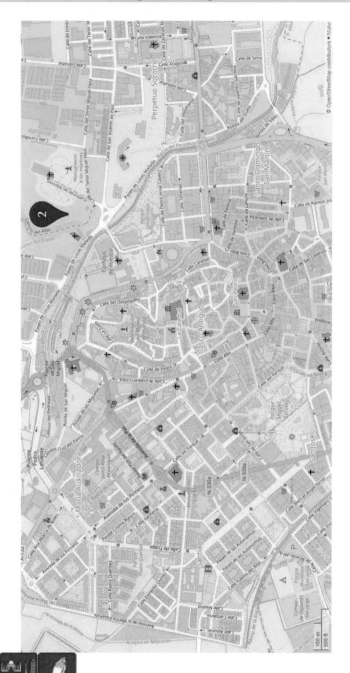

If you are driving, you can park near the Miguel Servet Park and start your visit by heading towards the historic center, by the pretty López Allué Square and the Monastery of San Pedro el Viejo, which is an old abbey , built in the 12th century in Roman Aragonese style. The rectangular cloister is surrounded by double columns with capitals illustrating the life of Jesus and allegorical scenes.

Photo 2.2: Plaza López Allué

Continuing 300 meters to the north you will arrive at the Cathedral of the *Seo de Santa María*. An imposing building of the thirteenth century in Gothic style, the cathedral is flanked by a steeple and the portal is decorated with beautiful sculptures of the apostles. The interior is quite austere. Returning to the center by walking through the alleys of the old town, you will come across another church - *Basílica de San Lorenzo*, dating from the seventeenth century, in Baroque style.

Photo 2.4: plaza Navarra

Do not miss the pretty Plaza Navarra on your way back to your starting point. In the middle of the square there is a beautiful fountain: Fuente de las Musas. Here you will also find the old Huesca Municipal Casino, a beautiful building built in the twentieth century looking like a small palace, where you can have a good coffee and pastry. Another beautiful building that borders the square is that of the Treasury.

You can end your visit with a walk in the city park: Parque Miguel Servet. There are shady alleys, a small lake with ducks, playgrounds for children. Charming!

If you are in Huesca for several days, I recommend a beautiful circuit of just over 200 km through the **Mallos de Riglos**, San Juan de la Peña, then by Jaca.

Photo 2.7: Castle-abbey of Loarre

From Huesca, head towards Loarre to see the magnificent Loarre Castle-Abbey 30 km to the north-west. It is a magnificent fortress of the eleventh century perched on a rocky peak at an altitude of over 1,000 meters where you will arrive by a winding road. The walled enclosure with 2 meter thick walls is flanked by 10 circular towers and the entrance door is narrow enough to prevent assailants from using rams and to facilitate its defense. You will be able to visit the complex which also includes several churches, the annexes of the monastery, the room and the court of arms, but also the crypt of *Santa Quiteria* and the mirador of the Queen which offers you a beautiful panorama on the province.

Photo 2.8: Castle-abbey of Loarre

From Loarre, follow the 1132 road through the *Mallos de Riglos*: magnificent rock formations that create a beautiful landscape with peaks over 300 meters high. The mallos are divided into two parts - the Big ones and the Small ones. This is a place that will delight climbing lovers. The road meanders along the Gallego River which has carved out gorges, forming magnificent landscapes.

Photo 2.9: Mallos de Riglos

Continuing your route, you will pass by the Monastery of San Juan de la Peña which seems encrusted in the rock. It was founded by Galindo II Aznárez, Earl of Aragon, in 920. The low church is one of the few remaining Mozarabic buildings in the area. The upper floor consists of a pantheon of Aragonese nobles, the royal pantheon and the high church built in the eleventh century. The cloister is wedged between the precipice and the cliff. Another Baroque-style monastery was built higher up in the 17th century and that's where you can park your car if you want to visit the monastery.

Photo 2.11: Monastery of San Juan de la Peña

A short stop at **Jaca** will make you discover the first capital of the kingdom of Aragon in the twelfth century, one of the starting points of the Reconquista. It is on the pilgrimage route Camino aragonés to Santiago de Compostelle.

By entering the narrow streets of the historic center you will discover pretty little squares bordered by beautiful houses. *San Pedro de Jaca* Cathedral was built in the 11th century in Romanesque style. The citadel of the city was built by Philip II in the sixteenth century and now houses the Museum of Military Miniatures with a collection of tens of thousands of soldiers. Not far away, another beautiful church is *Iglesia del Carmen* of the seventeenth century with a beautiful entrance topped with sculptures.

Photo 2.14: Citadel of Jaca

If you want to sleep in Huesca in the city center there is a nice hostel: Hostal Lizana with large rooms from 35 € per night for a double room

21

and with a very warm welcome. There is even a parking lot on site, but you have to pay extra. You can book on Booking.com because they have a website that does not always work ... Otherwise a great little hotel between Huesca and Zaragoza at a good value is called Casa Rural Marga. It is located in the small village of Tardienta. The rooms are comfortable and the double is from 40 € / night. The owner is very kind. You can book on the same website without problem.

If you want to eat in Huesca not far from the citadel, in the street *Calle Padre Huesca* there is a typical restaurant: Restaurante Comomelocomo, with hearty menus for about twenty euros and specialties and tapas to enjoy like boletus and liver risotto. Yum!

And if you come back from Jaca to Huesca, take the A23 road which offers beautiful landscapes, crosses many tunnels and passes over viaducts with superb views of the valleys. And if you are hungry, stop at the Monrepos station where you can get fuel, but also eat at reasonable prices. We tried a menu at 18 euros and their pork tenderloin is - really - very good. You will also be able to taste their tomasinas, a kind of pastries. They also offer rooms to spend the night. Convenient!

3. Alquézar, Ainsa, and Barbastro

Alquézar is a beautiful medieval village located in the Sierra de Guara on the Río Vero in the Natural Park of Sierra and Guara Gorge, less than 50 km northeast of Huesca and 120 km from Zaragoza. Alquézar is definitely worth a visit although it is very popular for tourists. Perched on a rocky outcrop, this fortified village with ocher tones will surprise you with its beauty that takes shape in a beautiful natural scenery

Do not be tempted to drive down to the village because the return will be difficult ;-). It is better to park in the large car parks at the top, then walk down to the village.

Photo 3.1: Alquézar

Let yourself be wandered through the narrow streets of the medieval fortified village, passing through the Plaza Mayor and up to the *Colegiata de Santa María la Mayor* of the 9th century. The Gothic and Romanesque cloister was added in the 14th century, later decorated with New Testament frescoes.

Photo 3.3: Alquézar

If you spend the summer and want to swim, you can do it below the village in the Rio Vero and you can also go on an aquatic descent of canyons. If you like climbing and even if you are a beginner, there is also a level 1 via ferrata in the Sierra de Guara. You can find here a company that organizes all these activities, but also rafting.

Photo 3.4: Alquézar

The Sierra Park and the Guara Canyons, with their magnificent rocky cliffs carved by water and breathtaking scenery are crisscrossed by hiking trails. You can see here several routes http://www.vertientesaventura.com/fr/sentiers-guara.html. I recommend a fairly easy hike - the Route des Passerelles or the Fuente Canyon which will take you less than two hours with spectacular views of the canyon.

If you want to eat in Alquézar, I recommend the terraces below where you have a breathtaking view of the village. They all have menus between 15 and 22 € for lunch and even if it's a bit like "the tourist factory", you can also fall on a good specialty. We tried La Cocineta and the menu at 15 €. The suckling pig of Segovia was good, as well as the Gaspacho.

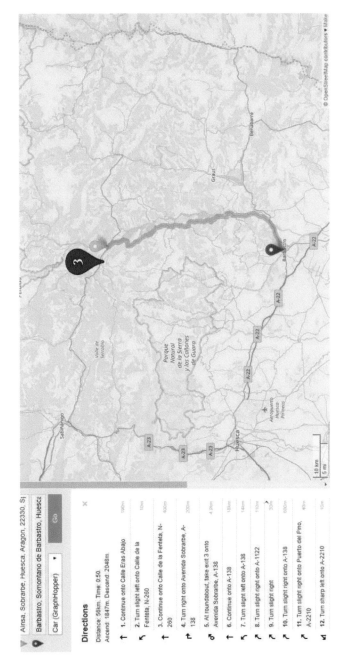

Ainsa, Sobrarbe, Huesca, Aragon, 22330, Sp

Barbastro, Somontano de Barbastro, Huesca

Car (GraphHopper) ▾   Go   ✕

Directions

Distance: 56km. Time: 0:50.
Ascend: 1847m. Descend: 2048m.

↑ 1. Continue onto Calle Eras Abajo   140m

↱ 2. Turn slight left onto Calle de la
Fenteta, N-260   10m

↑ 3. Continue onto Calle de la Fenteta, N-
260   490m

↱ 4. Turn right onto Avenida Sobrarbe, A-
138   200m

↻ 5. At roundabout, take exit 3 onto
Avenida Sobrarbe, A-138   4.2km

↑ 6. Continue onto A-138   19km

↰ 7. Turn slight left onto A-138   14km

↱ 8. Turn slight right onto A-1122   110m

↱ 9. Turn slight right   20m

↱ 10. Turn slight right onto A-138   600m

↱ 11. Turn slight right onto Puerto del Pino,
A-2210   40m

↲ 12. Turn sharp left onto A-2210   10m

Another visit worth seeing is the villages of **Ainsa, Morillo de Tou** and **Barbastro**.

Ainsa was the capital of the kingdom of Sobrarbe in the eleventh century before being incorporated into the Kingdom of Aragon.

Photo 3.5: Landscape from Ainsa

Ainsa is a small medieval village for which we had a real crush. Ainsa is less known and frequented than Alquézar, but the charm of its stone houses with flowery windows, narrow paved alleys, terraces, inns with the charm of yesteryear and an almost unreal serenity in the morning before tourists arrive, have completely conquered us. You will start the visit by the entrance of the city which is done on the narrow bridge which allowed the access to the fortified village. The Ainsa Castle, dating back to the 11th century, was part of the defensive line of the Christian territories and became a fortified city in the Middle Ages. There is only the tower Torre del Tenente, which today houses an Ecomuseum, the parade ground surrounded by a walkway and a gate that gives access to the Plaza Mayor.

Photo 3.6: Ainsa - Plaza Mayor

Arriving on the Plaza Mayor, the charm of this medieval village operates immediately with its beautiful gray stone houses and arched wooden beams. Continuing in the narrow streets of the village you will discover other beautiful buildings of the fourteenth century.

Photo 3.7: Ainsa - Plaza Mayor

Small squares, a green area with stone benches and each house that amazes by its simple beauty and attracts the eye with a beautiful window, a typical Aragonese fireplace, a pretty wooden door or a wrought iron decoration. You will then discover the collegiate church Santa Maria built from the eleventh century and completed two centuries later, in Aragonese Romanesque style, flanked by a bell tower.

You can continue the discovery to the south going to **Barbastro**.

Less than 5 km south of Ainsa you can make a short stop at **Morillo de Tou** which is actually a small medieval village turned into a campsite. An excellent initiative for the restoration and preservation of heritage that will allow you to discover the church of Santa Ana, dating from the seventeenth century, in Gothic-Cisterns style transformed into a museum and presenting the traditional Aragonese pottery. If you want to spend a few days in this amazing place, you can either install your tent or rent a bungalow or a cabin. You have everything on site - a library, a small supermarket, a swimming pool. For all the details, see their website here http://morillodetou.com/fr.

You can finish your tour by **Barbastro**, located about fifty kilometers south of Ainsa at the confluence of the rivers Cinca and Vero. It's a pretty little town with lively alleys, terraces and shops, a Gothic-style 16th century cathedral with a magnificent alabaster altarpiece, the nearby Episcopal Palace, and *Palacio de los Argensola* and the oldest square in the city *Plaza de la candelera*. For museum lovers there are some in the city, including the wine museum and the bulls museum.

Photo 3.10: Morillo de Tou

4. Teruel

Teruel is a city in the south of Aragon, capital of the province of the same name, located less than 200 kilometers south of Zaragoza. It is a city that deserves a small stop during your discovery of Aragon.

You can start your visit with its beautiful cathedral which is also the main attraction of Teruel, a very fine example of Mudéjar art whose construction began in the 12th century. Its beautiful Moorish tower of the 13th century is richly decorated with glazed ceramics. The facade was built in the twentieth century, in New-Mudejar style. Feel free to enter to discover its magnificent Mudejar coffered ceiling with paintings as well historical, religious as with fantastic creatures. The Mudejar dome of the cathedral enhances the beauty of the whole.

Photo 4.1: Cathedral of Teruel

The main square of the city is the *Plaza del Torico* with its column surmounted by a small black bull that gave the name to the square and represents the emblem of the city. The square is lined with lively terraces and small shops where you can spend a pleasant time drinking a coffee or a chocolate. This is where you can see also the beautiful house El Torico, built in the twentieth century.

Another gem of the city is its Tower of San Salvador, another superb example of Mudejar architecture, built in the fourteenth century and which you can visit. If you climb the tower you will have a breathtaking view of the city. On the other side of the cathedral square, a similar tower, Torre de San Martín built at the same time and in the same style. Both towers are part of UNESCO World Heritage as an example of Aragonese Mudejar art. Also take the grand staircase in New-Mudejar style that descends from the historic center down the city, built in the early twentieth century and which replicates the old Mudejar style with green colors, enameled escutcheons and two side turrets. The central part takes the famous scene of the lovers Diego and Isabel. Going down you can see the shady park and even go to enjoy its freshness.

If you are traveling with children, to the south-east of the city of Teruel there is a park that will please them: Dinópolis. It is a theme park with dinosaurs, mammoths, cave bears, which will take them back in time. It also houses a Paleontological Museum with fossils and life-size reproductions, as well as interactive and playgrounds for all ages. For more details, schedules and prices see their website here http://www.dinopolis.com/?lang=fr.

Spain: general presentation of the country

Spain, in long form, the Kingdom of Spain, in Castilian España is a country in southwestern Europe occupying most of the Iberian Peninsula.

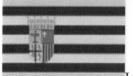

In this e-guide, we focus on the region: **Aragon**

Capital: Madrid

Geography: Surface: 505.911 km2

Population: around 46 millions inhabitants.

Spoken languages: Spanish or **Castilian** is the official language throughout Spain. There are other official languages in certain regions: **Basque** in the Basque Country and Navarre, **Catalan** in Catalonia, the Balearic Islands and in the Valencian Community, **Galician** in Galicia, and **Occitan Aranese** in Val d'Aran.

Currency: Euro.

Infrastructure: The Spanish road network is highly developed with more than 346,000 km of roads including 9,000 km of motorway. There are toll motorways, but there are also many highways that are still free of charge. The rail network is over 11,000 km and Madrid is connected by high-speed train to several cities. As for airports, Spain has over a hundred and more than a dozen Spanish airlines serve its airspace. For more details on transport in Spain see this article from Wikipedia.

Climate: There are three main climatic zones in Spain: the Mediterranean climate in the south and north-west of the country, the oceanic climate in the west of the country and the semi-arid climate in the south-east, which has a longer dry season, longer than summer.

History: The Iberians are developing at the beginning of the first millennium BC which ends with the Roman conquest in the second century BC. In the region that includes present-day Andalusia, around the Guadalquivir basin the Tartessian culture will develop, with a language, a writing, a culture and a social and political organization distinct from that of neighboring peoples, having a great Phoenician influence. In this Iberian settlement will be aggregated north and west Celtic populations, known as Celtiberians, from the thirteenth century BC.

From the 9th century BC, the Phoenicians create counters on the Mediterranean coast.

In -197, the Romans divide the Iberian territories into two provinces: Hispania Cited to the north, with Tarraco (Tarragona), as capital, and Hispania later to south, with its capital to Cordoba.

After 63 and until the fall of the Roman Empire, Augustus Caesar founded several Roman colonies for veterans like for example, Caesaraugusta (Zaragoza).

Vespasian (69-79) gave the Latin right to all the cities of Hispania, allowing access to Roman citizenship of the former magistrates of these cities and families of the Hispanic elite have gradually integrated into the Roman imperial elite. The Latin language is the language base of most languages spoken today in the Iberian Peninsula.

At the fall of the Roman Empire in the fifth century, German barbarians, Suevi, Vandals and Visigoths invaded Spain. Until the seventh century, the territory is inhabited by Gothi (Visigoths) the Hispano-Roman natives (Hispani). The Arab-Berbers led by Tariq ibn Ziyad conquered Spain in 711. In 756, Muslim Spain took its independence and in 929, the country became a caliphate. In the eleventh century, the caliphate fragmented into micro-states.

The political unification of present Spain began from the union of the Crowns of Castile and Aragon, by the marriage in 1469 of the heirs of these two states, the future Isabella Ire of Castile (1474-1504) and the future Ferdinand II of Aragon (1479-1516). In 1512, the Iberian part of the Kingdom of Navarre was added and the Conquistadors began to conquer vast territories to form a huge colonial empire.

The Spanish Inquisition, established in 1478 to maintain Catholic orthodoxy, fought against "New Christians", conversos (formerly forcibly converted Jews) and Moriscos, suspected of continuing to practice their religions of origin in hiding.

In the sixteenth century, the Habsburg Empire, whose Spanish Monarchy was, with the Holy Roman Empire, the essential element, became the first European power. In 1700, the grandson of Louis XIV from France, whose first wife was a Spanish Infanta, became King of Spain under the name of Philip V, and founded the dynasty of the Bourbons of Spain, bound by the Family Pact to Bourbons of France.

In 1808, Napoleon I invaded Spain and placed his brother Joseph Bonaparte on the throne.

Spain lost most of its colonies in the nineteenth century and a first republic was set up. The Second Spanish Republic brought down the monarchy of the Bourbons in 1931. The far right (Carlist and Phalangist) organized an uprising, subjecting Spain, after a tragic civil war from 1936 to 1939, to the dictatorship of General Franco. At his death, in 1975, the monarchy is restored and Juan Carlos I, the new king, quickly restores the representative democracy. If you want to know more about the turbulent history of Spain, see the article on Wikipedia.

Useful websites

History, geography: Wikipedia.
Tourism: An interesting site with a lot of information is to be found herehttp://www.spain.info/fr/.

Gastronomy

The Aragonese cuisine is rich by its varied influences and civilizations that have stayed on its territories. The products of the land are in the spotlight in this region, as are pork and cold cuts such as Teruel Ham, Longaniza and Fardeles. Lamb and suckling pig are also among the specialties

You can eat in the tapas bars or on the terraces where there are often menus of the day, but also in more chic restaurants if you have a larger budget.

Starters and soups: The starters you can eat in restaurants are often cold cuts with melon, mixed salads or meat, vegetable or seafood puff pastries. Soups are not consumed very often in Aragon, while in the old days the population ate soups made from sorrel, leeks, vermicelli, chicken broth, borage and other soups. You can nevertheless find the famous Spanish gaspacho of which you will find a recipe below.

The dishes: Migas is a typical Spanish dish, some of which are specific to Aragon, mainly made from garlic-flavored dry bread and cold meats. One of the Aragonese variants is garlic, chorizo and with grapes. One of Aragon's specialties is its braised milk lamb called " ternasco " accompanied by potatoes.

You can also try the cod "al ajoarriero" which is a dish of cod fried with garlic then mixed with potatoes, onions and eggs. The Chilindrón chicken is perhaps the most typical of the Aragonese cuisine with its tomato, onion, garlic, red pepper and ham sauce. The "*fritada aragonesa*" is another typical dish made of potatoes, zucchini, onions, red and green peppers accompanied by tuna or snails.

Desserts: One of the traditional desserts of Aragon is the Crespillos which are small donuts made from fried borage leaves. Another delicacy of the region is the " Guirlache ", a kind of nougat made from almonds and sugar, but also yemas of Aragon (a confectionery), the tortas de balsa and those with honey.

To travel while staying in your kitchen or extend your experience in Spain, here are some recipes to make at home and bring some of the Aragonese gastronomy back with you.

Migas de pan

- 4 slices of dry bread, 1 chorizo, 1 box of bacon, 100 g bacon
- 2 cloves of garlic, 1 tomato, olive oil, paprika, salt pepper

Crumble the bread and put it in a damp cloth overnight. In a frying pan put a splash of oil and fry the bacon and sliced chorizo. Reserve them. In the same pan put garlic cut into pieces with bread and a little paprika. Add salt and pepper to your taste and diced tomato. Put back the sausages, stirring for a few minutes over a low heat. Serve hot with fresh vegetables or grapes.

Gaspacho

- 1 cucumber, 7 ripe tomatoes, 1 clove of garlic, 1 red pepper, 1 yellow pepper
- 2 green onions, some fresh basil leaves, olive oil, 1 tablespoon of vinegar

Wash all vegetables and basil. Peel the cucumber and cut it into pieces. Cut the peppers into large slices and the tomatoes in half. Peel the garlic and cut it finely, as well as the green onion. Put everything in the robot and mix. Add olive oil and vinegar. Place the soup in the fridge for several hours. Serve the soup with finely chopped basil leaves.

Chicken "a la chilindrón"

- 1 chicken, 2 slices of ham, 2 cloves garlic, 1 onion
- 4 tomatoes, 2 red peppers, olive oil, salt

Wash and cut the chicken. In a large skillet, brown the garlic in a little olive oil, then add the chicken pieces and turn over when golden brown.

Meanwhile, wash the tomatoes, onion and pepper. Cut the tomatoes into dices, peppers into strips and chop the onion. Add to the skillet the chopped ham, onion and peppers. Cook for a few minutes, mixing.

Add the tomatoes and cook over low heat until the sauce is well preserved.

Crespillos of Borage

A dessert recipe easy to make.
- 100 g borage leaves and stems, 50 ml of milk, 100g of flour
- 3 eggs, 1 packet of vanilla sugar, 1 pinch of baking powder, olive oil

Wash and dry the borage. In a bowl, beat the eggs with flour and yeast. Add milk and sugar while stirring. The dough should be quite thick. In a pan, heat the oil. Dip the leaves in the dough and then dip spoons of dough into the oil. Leave to brown then return. Take out on paper towels.

Lamb with potatoes

- 1 leg of lamb, 1 onion, 5-6 potatoes
- paprika, 100 ml red wine, salt pepper

For the marinade: 4 tablespoons of olive oil, a few parsley leaves, finely chopped sage, thyme and savory, 2 cloves of finely chopped garlic. Mix all ingredients. Wash the leg and dry it. Put the leg of lamb in a baking dish, season with salt and pepper and coat with marinade. Wash and peel potatoes and onions, slice and arrange around leg. Put the wine by basting the meat.

Bake in the preheated oven and water the leg with the sauce regularly. Cook for over an hour over low heat until the lamb is tender. Enjoy your meal!

Spanish travel lexicon

While traveling around the world, I realized that in some countries it is not easy to cope if one does not know the language and if the natives do not speak a foreign language. I thought then that a little "travel" lexicon would be very useful not only to be courteous (say Hello, Thank you, Goodbye), but also to know what to order at the restaurant. So I hope that my little travel lexicon will be useful to you to manage during your trip!

Politeness and essential expressions / words

Hello! - **¡Buenos días!** (read: buenos dias) and in the afternoon **¡Buenas tardes!**
Bye! - **¡Hasta luego!** (asta louego) or **Adios**
Good evening! - **¡Buenas noches!**
Please - **Por favor**
Excuse-me - **Perdona**
Yes- **sì**   No - **no**
Thank you very much - **Muchas gracias**
How are you? - **¿Qué tal?**
Do you speak english? **¿Habla inglés?** (abla ingles)
I don't understand - **Perdón**
I don't know - **No lo sé (**no lo sé**)**
Sorry (to excuse somebody) -**Perdón**
Sorry (to pass) -**Con permiso**
Hospital - **hospital**
Pharmacy - **farmacia**
Bank - **banco**
Supermarket - **supermercado**
Street - **calle**
Doctor - **Médico doctor**

*I preferred to write a "proper" phonetic transcription because official phonetic signs are not always easy to remember ;-), but you can also hear the pronunciation on the google website for example.

Restaurant

Menu - menú   (meniu) or carta
Eat - comer
Breakfast - El desayuno (el dessailluno)
The bill please! - ¡La cuenta por favor!
Drink - bebida
Water – agua   Wine – Vino   Beer – cerveza

Bread - pan
Salt – sal   Pepper -pimienta
Mustard– mostaza
Soup - sopa
Salad - ensalada
Meat – carne   Pork - carne de cerdo   Beef - carne de res
Chicken – pollo   Fish – pescado   Sea food - mariscos
French fries - Patatas fritas
Vegetables - verduras
Rice - arroz
Pasta – pastas
Sausages -salchichas
Potatoes - patatas
Cheese - queso
Dessert - postre
Ice cream - helado
Bean -frijoles
orange juice -zumo de naranja
Enjoy your meal! - ¡Buen provecho!

To the hotel

Do you have free rooms? -¿Tiene alguna habitación disponible?
double room -habitación doble
single room -habitación individual
bathroom -cuarto de baño
shower -ducha
What is the price of one night? - ¿Cuál es el precio de una noche? (cual es el pressio de una notché)
Can I see the room first please? -¿Podría echar un vistazo a la habitación, por favor?
key- clave (clavé)

Numbers

0 –cero   8 -ocho
1 - un (ouno)   9 -nueve (nuebé)
2 -dos (dos)   10 - diez
3 -tres (tres)   11 -once
4 -quatro (quatro)   12 -doce (dossé)
5 -cinco (sinko)   19 -diecinueve (diéssinuebé)
6 -seis   20 -veinte
7 –siete   21 - veintiuno...
30 -treinta (treynta)   40 -cuarenta
50 -cincuenta   60 -sesenta
70 -setenta   100 -cien   1000 –mil

On the road and in the city

Parking -estacionamiento
Station -estación
Airport -aeropuerto
Bus -autobús
Train - tren
Round-trip ticket - Billete de ida y vuelta
Gas station -Estación de servicio
Entry –entrada   Exit -salida
Attention –atención   Forbidden -prohibido
straight ahead -recto
Turn left -Gire a la izquierda   Turn right -Gire a la derecha
Toilets -baños
How much does it cost? - ¿Cuánto cuesta ?
It's too expensive! : Es demasiado caro

HOW TO GET THE EBOOK FOR FREE

Did you appreciate this paperback ?
Would you like to have an electronic version of it, for free ?
You could then have it on your smartphone, electronic reader or Kindle, always at hand!
It is easy: just send me an email with a proof of your purchase (this paperback) and I will send the file right away, into your inbox!
For that, simply use my email address: cristina.rebiere@gmail.com
  Hoping to read from you soon ☺

                                                    Cristina

Credits

We thank Wikipedia et OpenStreetMap websites for the free resources used in the development of this guide (photographs and maps). We are grateful to all contributors to these sites without whom we would not be able to complete some of our articles. Also thanks to all the kind souls who offer online tools and free resources to use for those who still want to learn and improve!

Photo credits:
Photo 2.11: De Sergio - San Juan de la Peña, CC BY 2.0
Photo 4.1,3: De Diego Delso, CC BY-SA 3.0
Photo 4.2: De igorre1969 - originally posted to Flickr as Teruel, CC BY-SA 2.0

Authors

Cristina & Olivier Rebière met at the age of 17 in 1990 in Romania, shortly after the fall of the Berlin Wall and the Romanian Revolution of December 1989. After two years of correspondence and several meetings, Cristina was able to get a scholarship to study in France and became Olivier's wife in 1993. Since then, these two "life adventurers" have had an existence full of twists and turns, during which they fell in love with travel, entrepreneurship and writing.

Their books are useful, practical, and will fill you up with energy and creativity. In addition to your practical guides of this collection, discover other ebooks by Cristina & Olivier on their website **http://www.OlivierRebiere.com**

Printed in Great Britain
by Amazon